T0392280

BLESSED
BEYOND
MEASURE

LAUREN GRANT

WESTBOW
PRESS®
A DIVISION OF THOMAS NELSON
& ZONDERVAN

To my beloved grandma, who showed me the way

After you have suffered for a little while, the God of grace, who called you to his eternal glory in Christ, will Himself, perfect, confirm, strengthen and establish you.

—1 Peter 5:10

My cup overflows with Your blessings.

—Psalm 23:5

CONTENTS

CONTENTS

INTRODUCTION

Those who have known me all my life will react to my story in different ways: pity, astonishment, guilt, and disbelief—that is, until I begin to share the details of my life with others and how God transformed me.

It is amazing how God uses His great powers to protect us. In my case, He caused my body to suppress the pain that I had suffered while growing up.

I recall one day when I was in my midforties and was cheerfully vacuuming the carpet. Out of the blue, a series of flashbacks of the abuse my mother heaped upon me filled my mind. The images were so vivid that they felt like they happened yesterday.

I believe that my gracious Lord allowed these memories to be released from my brain at that time because I was finally able to process them. It was a very painful emotional process, and I screamed at these terrible images, but I soon was able to become calm again.

In this book, I will detail some of my experiences while I was growing up and how these came to affect the rest of my life.

But before I go any further, I must tell you that I did experience moments of happiness, and most of these happened when my family lived on the farm. I will share with you some of these in the final chapter.

I must warn the reader that this is not a pretty story, and it is difficult to tell, but it is also a story of grace, redemption, hope, and joy.

LOST

My earliest memory is of being assaulted by a relative in his truck when I was four years old.

That traumatic memory has never left me. When I was seventy years old, I was watching a movie at home with my husband, and the opening scene featured a truck that I recognized immediately. It was the same make, model, and color of the truck from that awful day.

I ran from the room, choking down tears and feeling pressure over my heart. After a while, I came back into the room and told my husband what had just happened to me.

He jumped out of his chair and took me into his arms, all the while saying, "Oh, honey, I am so sorry."

When you are a survivor of childhood abuse, you never "get over it," but if you are fortunate, you learn to manage those memories and not allow them to manage your life.

> The light shines in the darkness and
> the darkness can never extinguish it.
>
> —John 1:5

TWO

GROWING UP WITH MAMA

THE BEATINGS

I grew up as a young child suffering from many years of beatings at the hands of my mother. The reasons for her rage remain a mystery. I learned to cope by trying to occupy as little space in the world as possible and to avoid her whenever I could. She only abused me when we were alone, and now I believe this was because she did not want any witnesses. My brothers and my dad never knew this was going on even though she was beating my sister as well.

To avoid serious damage, I would curl up into a fetal position to protect my body from the hard lashings of the belt and having my hair pulled out. Mama would only stop the blows when she was too exhausted to go on. Then, she would scream at me, "Get out! It makes me sick to look at you! You disgust me!"

I also recall when she was "helping" me with my arithmetic homework that each time I gave the wrong answer to a problem, she would slap me hard across the face. This went on until my face was badly swollen, and then she sent me to bed. By this time, it was almost midnight, and I had school the following morning. I was still exhausted, and my mind seemed numb.

When Mama would beat me, I was so frightened that I could not speak; I only endured the blows. With my dear, sweet sister, it was a different experience. She would always try to fight back—striking back, screaming, biting, and scratching—but Mama was much stronger than my sister, so it only made matters worse for her. Many times, when she finished battering her, Mama would pick up the small body of my sister and throw her into a cramped crawl space under the stairs. She would lock her inside it, and my sister would remain there for hours with no food, water, or bathroom breaks.

What my mother was doing to us was actually torture. There is simply no other term for it.

Enduring this physical and emotional abuse had such an effect on me that I failed the eighth grade.

> But blessed are those who trust in the LORD
> and have made the LORD their hope.
> —Jeremiah 17:7

Even as a young girl, I have always been drawn to the beauty of nature, but now that I think back on it, perhaps God was preparing me for what lay ahead.

We lived on a farm that had a creek flowing through it. This became my sanctuary for healing.

Little did I realize that God was holding my hand during all the abuse. I know this because He did not allow any permanent physical damage to occur. The welts and lacerations eventually healed, although my spirit was broken, and emotional scarring was the result.

When I was in the eighth grade, I was called into the principal's office. When I entered the quiet office, I saw that both of my parents were there. I became terrified because my parents had never been to my school before except to enroll me. I feared what physical torment my mother would heap on me as a result of meeting with "people outside our family."

The principal asked me to sit down—away from my parents—and then he did an extraordinary thing. He looked my mama straight in the eye and said, "I do not know what is going on at your house, but it stops today."

Apparently, someone had reported her as I had been to school recently with evidence of the physical abuse she had given me that morning before I got on the school bus.

In defense of my daddy, I truly believe that he was not aware of the beatings because they always happened when he was at work.

She never physically abused me again. I repeated the grade and made excellent marks because I could now concentrate on my studies.

Although she never physically abused me again, the verbal abuse continued into high school. She often told me how ugly and unintelligent I was and that no man would ever love me. Another devastating experience I recall was when I was lamenting that I had never been to a homecoming dance or a prom. My mother quipped, "You are so ugly and ignorant, no man will ever want you." I was crushed. When you hear this enough times, you eventually begin to believe it, and I did. The thing about being abused physically and verbally as a child is that it affects you psychologically for the rest of your life.

While I was finally free of the physical abuse, she now began to abuse Walter, one of my twin brothers. He had swallowed some nuts and bolts when he was two and a half years old. For some reason, instead of going into his stomach, they went into his lungs. As a result, he had one lung and a portion of the other removed. Mama delighted in pushing my brother to the floor where she would sit on his chest—laughing the whole time. Walter would panic and scream, "I can't breathe!" All of us kids were crying and trying to pull her off him. She did this many times, but the last time she did it was when Warren, my brother's identical twin, had enough of this and screamed at her, "I know I am just a little kid, but I will find a way to kill you if you do that again!" She got the message and stopped doing this. My hero brother was only eight years old at the time. He was so brave.

I always envied other girls for having mothers who loved and cared about them. My self-esteem suffered greatly, and I was beyond shy because Mama had broken my spirit.

One of Mama's friends confided to her (unaware of the real reason for my extreme shyness) that taking voice lessons sometimes develops a person's confidence. She gave Mama the name and phone number of a voice teacher she knew. Mama told me (not asked) that I would be taking voice lessons to possibly help with my lack of self-confidence. The teacher turned out to be a warm, lovely woman who was a former opera singer. As we began to vocalize (my first experience with this), she wanted to discover my range. As she played, the scale notes went higher and higher. After a while, she excused herself, saying that she needed to make a phone call.

That phone call was to my mother. The teacher exclaimed to her, "You didn't tell me that your daughter could sing!"

Mama was dumbfounded. "What? She can?"

That is when we learned that my voice (and my now-emerging interest) was well suited to opera, and my teacher began to teach me many arias and other classical works. I was thrilled! The higher the notes were, the more my happiness soared as I sang with joy. One day, I went in for my lesson, and the teacher confided that she had taught me all she knew and it was time for me to go further in my studies.

In my senior year of high school, I told my parents that I wanted to go to college. They both looked startled, and after a long pause, they announced, "Well, we are not going to pay for it, so we sure hope you have the money!" I had some money saved from working at two previous summer jobs but was finally forced to sell my beloved horse to come up with the funds.

I applied to a small local college and was accepted. After I graduated from high school, I attended for a while but then discovered that this school did not offer the type of musical education I needed for my voice major. This would require a specialized education that is only offered at a music conservatory as my aspiration was to become an opera singer. As I did research into this area, my hopes were dashed because the cost of such an education was well beyond my reach. What I truly needed was a mentor to help me. I had very little money left and no encouragement or guidance from my parents, so I dropped out of school, and my vocal education stopped there.

I did continue to sing, however, in the evenings and on weekends. I sang in my church choir and as a guest soloist at the air force base's chapel. I also sang with my hometown's civic chorus.

Another bright spot in my life at this time was teaching a Sunday-school class to four-year-olds. How I loved being with those children! My love for young children would remain with me all my life.

Now that I was no longer a student, it was time for me to get a full-time job. My first one was as a long-distance telephone operator. I enjoyed the work, and my supervisor was just about to give me a raise and a promotion when a most unexpected turn of events happened while I was at work.

THE GRAND FARCE

While I was busy at work one day, my supervisor came up to me and called out my name, and when I saw her facial expression, I immediately knew something was very wrong. She took me to her office and told me that my mama had tried to end her life. An ambulance had been called, and through swift medical attention, her life was spared.

My supervisor gave me a slip of paper with an address I did not know and told me I could find Mama there. That was all she said.

When I drove to the address, I became even more frightened; it was a mental institution! When I entered the facility, I found a nurse to help me locate Mama's room. Just as I was about to push the door open, I heard laughter coming from inside the room. I thought that I had been given the wrong room number by mistake, but I recognized the voices. I opened the door and found Mama and my sister giggling and having a fine time.

Despite the fact that I saw such perplexing behavior, I ran to her bedside and hugged her. "Mama, what happened?" I asked her. She began to tell me a story that was, even for Mama, quite unbelievable.

Daddy had been placed on the night shift at work and was no longer there to help her raise my twin brothers who were now teens and quite a handful! When Daddy asked to be placed back on the day shift so Mama would have his stronger influence on my brothers, he was told that it would only happen due to an emergency. So my mother and my sister created one!

For once, I stood up to her and, with all the courage I could muster, questioned her judgment. Her plan might have backfired and might have resulted in her death.

She told me that the reason I was not told of their plan was because I would not go along with it and spoil everything. She said that she knew exactly how many pills to take to get the job done.

I felt shocked and betrayed and suddenly realized how unstable my home life had become and that I was powerless to stop the decline of my family.

Meanwhile, I was discouraged with my job at the phone company because of the shift I worked and the pay, so I started looking for a better job. Luckily, I found a position that I enjoyed a great deal: a job in an upscale women's clothing store.

My work entailed monitoring each piece of clothing and the accessories (scarves, jewelry, etc.) that my employers sold in all three of their stores. It was detailed work, and I thrived in the highly organized environment it required. The hours flew by, and it was such a pleasure to be surrounded by all those beautiful things and the kind people working with me in the store.

The fashion buyer there encouraged me to think about becoming a buyer also. She told me that I had a "good eye for quality." The merchandise carried in the stores resembled Ralph Lauren's genre of goods.

While I was pondering a possible career in fashion, a chance meeting with someone would alter the remainder of my life in ways I could not imagine.

Here is something you should know about my daddy. While my daddy was a wonderful man in many ways, he seemed more like a friend to me and offered little advice or guidance in my life.

As you have seen, I did not grow up with the love and approval of my parents.

A SHOCKING ACCUSATION

I was twenty-one years old, working, attending church, being respectful, and trying to become the person God wanted me to be. I didn't drink, smoke, or do drugs, nor was I sexually promiscuous. You would think that having a daughter like me would be enough.

But nothing was good enough for my mother. Living at home became intolerable under her hateful and judgmental eye, so I decided to move out.

A friend from work and I planned to be roommates and get an apartment near our workplace. Her parents were supportive and even encouraging to us. They lovingly called us "young women of fine character." However, when I mentioned our plan to Mama, she sneered and told me that I must be a lesbian to move in with another woman. She admitted that she had not observed any sexual leanings in that direction but still made that conclusion because of my wanting to live with my friend—that was her rationale. This accusation made me change my mind about moving out.

It became clear to me that what she wanted was for me to remain at home and take care of her and Daddy and to deny me a life free from her.

Almost two years later, I was desperate to get away. I felt I had no other way out except to get married. How naive and foolish I was. I was about to complicate my life even further.

Before I talk about anything else, I need to introduce my grandma—my mother's mother. She was the exact opposite of my mother in temperament—never critical or suspicious in nature but a trusting and encouraging soul.

Here lies the conundrum. As a general rule, whenever someone has been abused as a child, they will become an abusive parent when they grow up. I do not believe that was the case with my grandmother. (It was not the case for me either.)

Whenever Grandma was in our presence, Mother treated her with respect and kindness. Whenever Grandma was not with us, Mother never mentioned that she or her siblings were abused by Grandma.

THREE

GRANDMA

Unwaveringly supportive and ever loving, my grandma was the most important person in my life while I was growing up. It is ironic that I became very much like her: soft-spoken, reserved, and having a deep regard and respect for the power of nature—especially flowers.

Most of all, she introduced me to Jesus, and she lived her life as an example of His teachings. She gave me my first Bible.

My guaranteed bright spot of the year was spending an entire week alone with her in her home. We spent the week with her teaching me about gardening. She made me an old-fashioned sun bonnet for me to wear to protect my skin while we were out in her garden. It looked exactly like the ones worn on the television series *Little House on the Prairie*. I learned about composting, and her dahlias were the size of dinner plates! I soaked it all in and was always ready to learn more from her. With her, no question was silly or ill-timed. That tiny woman had such a huge heart. She was a beacon of kindness, peace, comfort, and rest for me.

She was my angel on earth, and everything we did together that week—from picking wild huckleberries in the nearby woods to walking to see the local waterfall—was magical and such a grand adventure for me! We also went to her church (she called it Meeting), read scriptures, prayed, and sang hymns a cappella. I loved it because it was much like the early church of the New Testament.

We took a nap every day, sleeping together in her old saggy bed. Before we would nap, I would ask her about how her life was while she was growing up, and I will never forget what she said to me.

She told me that she had no recollection of her early childhood: her parents, her siblings, her name, and even her age. Her first memory was of her walking on a dusty country road. Many people did this at that time in the rural parts of the South. This happened in the late 1890s or early 1900s, but I am only guessing here.

She was "taken in" by a family, and they told her she looked to be about twelve years old. They gave her a home but worked her hard like a servant. Several years later, they sold her to a stranger who eventually married her and gave her his name. She suffered seven miscarriages, but eventually, she was able to carry three babies to term. My mother was the youngest one.

When Mama was about six months old, my grandpa was murdered. He went out to hunt one day, and two days later, his dog came back without him. That was a bad omen because those two were inseparable. Grandma sent her son out to search for him, and he found him dead on a trail with an ax buried in his skull. Grandpa was a deputy sheriff during the day and a moonshiner the rest of the time. His illegal deeds had finally caught up with him.

With three children to raise and feed, she took in washing from people. She used a huge iron pot in the yard; she boiled the clothes with drawn well water and lye soap, scrubbed them on her metal washboard to remove the stains, and dried them on a clothesline. She would then fold and deliver the laundry, and many times, she did the ironing too. Another thing she would do to raise money was sell the eggs her hens would lay.

She never married again, so she was forced to work extraordinarily hard. She was a single mother who did not drive or have a telephone. Her house did not have running water or electricity, so there was no air-conditioning or central heating. Also, there was no indoor plumbing, and cooking was done on a wood stove. Her kids took turns chopping wood for it and also helped Grandma can the produce she grew to keep them fed.

She taught herself to read and write since she only went to school for three days because her adopted family needed her to work for them and told her that "it was foolish for a girl to learn all that anyway."

When I think back on my hardships, I realize they were nothing compared to Grandma's life journey, but she still took the time to honor God, attend her church, and spread the Word of God.

Whenever I read this scripture in the Old Testament, I think of her.

> Those who are wise will shine as bright as the sky
> and those who lead many to righteousness will shine
> like the stars forever.
>
> —Daniel 12:3

She is still shining in my heart, and I look forward to meeting her in heaven.

FOUR

FROM THE FRYING PAN INTO THE FIRE

MARRIAGE

Disco was the rage in the 1960s, so a friend from work and I went to the grand opening of a new one. There, I met a young man named Kevin, who seemed nice and was interested in me.

He was kind and attentive to me. A few months later, he proposed, and I accepted. When he took me back to Alabama to meet his parents, his dad was friendly, but his mother was icy toward me. I got through the weekend there, and we decided to get married a few months later. I thought his mother would grow to love and accept me.

I guess I was too hopeful as the war against me began on the evening before our wedding. When the wedding party arrived in Virginia, where I was living at the time, my fiancé's wedding attire was wrong! We had decided that he and his groomsmen would be wearing black tuxedos. He sheepishly admitted to me that his mother thought that white dinner jackets would look better, so she had switched them!

I was never consulted, and the entire marriage continued to be a battle between us. My future husband always—without exception—agreed with his mother. His reason? He said that we should just let her have her way because she would not live very long. Really? She lived to be almost a hundred!

MISERY IN MARRIAGE

We were married for a short time when he told me that he had bought a necklace to give to an employee at his office's Christmas party and wanted my opinion of it. It was a pretty Chinese enameled pendant on a chain, and I said, "This is so pretty. I would love something like this myself." Years later, I found out that it was for one of his mistresses.

Other than my engagement and wedding rings, I never received jewelry from him for the entire time that we were together. As a matter of fact, he never gave me gifts (or cards) to celebrate my birthday, Christmas, or our anniversary! The only exception happened on our first wedding anniversary; his gift to me was something he actually wanted.

We never took a vacation without his mother traveling with us, and even then, it was only to see relatives.

There were no dinners out for the two of us. In fact, there was no going out at all.

One time, we had our best friends visiting from out of town. Baby Kyle was just a few months old at the time, and Ellen wanted to go shopping. Her husband loved kids, so he volunteered to babysit so we could go. We had a wonderful time, but I learned many years later that when my husband changed the baby's messy diaper, instead of putting it in the diaper pail, he threw the cloth diaper down the basement steps! My friend's husband asked him why he did that, and my husband laughed and said, "That's OK. Lauren will clean it up when she gets home."

He would not allow me to use disposable diapers. He said that they would cause me to become lazy and they were too expensive anyway.

In the final year of our marriage, he not only refused to visit my family in Virginia but also refused to go to my dad's funeral and didn't want me to go either. Can you imagine?

SIGNS OF TROUBLE

Our journey to parenthood began on one of our wedding anniversaries, which he never celebrated with a card or a gift. I told him the best gift I could ever have was to go off the pill and become pregnant. He agreed. It took seventeen months for me to get pregnant.

When I found out that I was going to have a baby, I was beside myself with joy! I couldn't wait to tell him that night, so I called him at work and told him the news. I will never forget what he did next. There was a very long pause on his end of the phone, and then he coldly said, "Congratulations. I'm very happy for you."

What? He made it sound like I had gotten a job promotion.

Even after all these years. I truly believe that he never wanted kids. He never took them anywhere except to the local fire department (he was a volunteer there) so he could show them off—all cute and dressed up. He did not go to doctor appointments, school conferences, plays, etc. Basically, I was a single parent even though I was married. I now believe that the only reason he agreed to have children was because his mother was pressuring him to make her a grandmother. After the boys were born, he resented the time and attention I gave to them. He didn't realize that if he had shared in the parental responsibilities, I would have had more time to spend with him.

MISSING IN ACTION

When I became pregnant with our second son, Kevin was still not interested in being a parent, but I didn't want my first son to grow up alone, so he agreed to us having another child. I was so happy to be a mother. While their dad decided to miss out on the joys of his children, I was the opposite. I was with them when they went swimming, went on trips to the zoo, had playdates, had library-fun days, etc.

When I was heavily pregnant with our second son and because my hairstyle was short (his idea, not mine) and my tummy was very large, he mocked me by telling me that I looked like a bowling pin—small top and large middle. With my confidence already low, that really stung. I felt shame and thought I was the ugliest woman around.

As I was about to give birth to our second son, Kevin could not be found anywhere. The hospital staff finally listened to me because I knew where he was. They called the sheriff in the county where he was working that day. The sheriff not only found him, but he also escorted him to the labor room due to the emergency situation. Years later, I learned that he was with his mistress as I was about to give birth to his child.

As our marriage was breaking up, there was one episode that I can still vividly recall. Our little boys and I were in the car and getting ready to go somewhere when their dad began to act very irrationally. His behavior was so odd and menacing that I became very frightened for our safety. I sped away as he was chasing us down our long driveway and screaming at the car.

I had no idea where to go as this was completely unplanned, but I knew I needed a friend right then. The boys felt very close to my friend Vivian, so I began the long drive to her house. I have no memory of that drive. Only when she opened the door did I seem to come to myself.

Here's the thing: her home was forty-five minutes away, and I had to drive up a mountain to get there; the roads were winding and treacherous! It has been almost forty years since that day, and I still have no recollection of that drive! I believe that God sent a guardian angel to protect us that day.

When the inevitable came and I was about to leave my husband, I was gathering up my belongings for our big move when I made a startling discovery. There were many photos of the boys, but I was not in any of them because I was always the photographer. Even when we visited my husband's parents, no photos were taken of me with the boys. Makes you wonder, doesn't it? Were his parents planning to remove me from my sons' lives all along? I'll never know as both have passed on now.

There was another issue (in addition to the apathy and the neglect) that we could not agree on, and that was going to church. He did not want me to go or to take the boys with me. I still took them, but whenever we got home, it was always very unpleasant because he could not control me.

ABSOLUTE POWER

It seemed that unless something I wanted was his idea, it had no value. He almost always opposed it and browbeat me about it. I was made to feel like a failure for even considering such an idea. This was his hold over me, and I felt trapped.

Here are some examples that are still vivid memories for me:

I wanted to go back to school and get a teaching degree, and a friend offered to finance my education. She had seen me teach the children in my class (I was a second-grade teaching assistant) and told me that I was a natural teacher. The children's teacher was frequently absent due to poor health and asked me to use her lesson plans.

I was so excited to discuss it with my husband because I was certain he would approve as we desperately needed the additional income. He completely blindsided me with this statement: "If you do this, I will divorce you." I never mentioned it again.

Another example is that I wanted to play tennis, and when I tried to discuss it with him, he criticized and shamed me by telling me that I was too uncoordinated to play (since I had never even held a racket, how did he know that?). To his thinking, this was yet another ridiculous idea, so I dropped it.

I feel now that he wanted to isolate me from other couples because I would learn that our relationship was unhealthy if I saw other couples who were balanced, respectful, and normal.

I think that all these things were indicators of his upbringing. When I saw firsthand how cold his parents were—especially to each other and to him—I realized this spousal model was what he adopted in our marriage as well. The husband was always in control, and his word was absolute and final.

Going back to the tennis example, after I left my husband to begin a new and healthier life, I took tennis lessons, and guess what? I became quite good at it and played on three tennis teams.

I truly believe in my heart that God helped me with this, and I thank Him daily for His guidance and for helping me not to become bitter.

Many times, he would gaslight me, but I did not know the term then. He constantly told me that I was worthless, couldn't learn new things, wasn't capable, and was not attractive. Sound familiar? Mama's method of controlling me was at work again.

Only when I left him and began dating again did I realize that none of those things were true, and I began to blossom. But my life truly began when I met my husband, Bill, who loved me (and still does more than thirty-nine years later) unconditionally. I had only felt this from my grandma and my children, so for another adult to do so was foreign to me. This is how Jesus sees us and thinks of us. But I did not know this at that time.

> For we are God's masterpiece. He has created us anew in Christ Jesus, so we can do good things he planned for us long ago.
> —Ephesians 2:10

An Unexpected Ally

Because I was kept isolated from Kevin's work environment, I did not know anyone from his office. This was his plan all along. This way, I could not be aware of his whereabouts or activities.

When our oldest son was only a month old, my husband came home from the office very excited and announced he was going on an outdoor office event with the other families. He did not include me, nor did he ask if I wanted to come along. When he said that it would involve rafting down a river over rapids, I begged him for many days to let me come also. He finally relented and agreed that I could come along.

When the day finally came, we were divided into groups of four to a raft. Many people were quite surprised to see me there but warmed up to me as we got into the rafts and shoved off. It was so exciting! The day was cool (the air in the mountains was chilly even though it was June), the water was dark green and sparkling, and the rapids were thrilling!

On one of the quiet lulls, I used my oar to push us away from a large rock. I didn't realize though that just below the surface of the water, the rock was covered with algae, and my oar slipped. *Splash*! I lost my balance and fell into that cold water, and it was deep. As I was struggling to catch my breath, I heard a man yell, "Someone help her! She can't get back in the raft!" I felt a hard pull on my arms; someone lifted me into the raft. As I was shivering in the raft, a stranger gave me his jacket, and I learned he was the one shouting for help and the one who rescued me. My husband did neither!

The man introduced himself to me, and he later told me that when I went overboard, my husband made no effort to help me. He thought, *That poor girl needs a friend*, and he did become a dear family friend for many years. When I left my marriage, he and a couple who also became my good friends helped me move from Alabama to Virginia on Christmas Eve. These three friends were Christians, and they all lived their faith that day.

I still find it amazing how God sends us just who we need when we are trying to survive and sometimes lack courage.

Wait on the LORD; be of good courage, and He shall
strengthen your heart; Wait, I say, on the LORD.
—Psalm 27:14

BETRAYAL

Regarding my marriage, as it turned out, I did not choose well (of course). I know now that my new husband was not the man I thought he was. He was verbally abusive at times and gaslighted me at others. I had taken a vow before God to be a good wife to him and to be a good mother to our precious little boys, so I stayed in the marriage for the children. As long as their dad traveled for business, I could manage our lives.

Things eventually came to a head when something I never expected happened.

On our wedding anniversary, Kevin was on a business trip, but this time, he did not call or come home. He came home the following day as if nothing was amiss. He told me that we had grown apart, but I had done nothing wrong. He hung his head in remorse as he said these things to me.

It was quite a performance. It was so good that I thought his guilt was genuine. Thank goodness we discussed this after our sons had fallen asleep.

I later learned that he was having an affair and was with his mistress on the night of our anniversary. I had often wondered where all our money was going. I later learned that he was spending it on his mistress. I told him that I would be willing to stay married to him if he would give her up and attend counseling with me.

He would not admit to the affair or agree to any of those terms, and he silently left the following day. He was gone for a week without a word.

I had become worried (he was the father of my children after all). So I phoned his mother to see if she had heard from him.

Oh, she had. He was staying with her, and she had gotten him an attorney. She had learned of the affair before I did, and she acted as if it were a normal thing. Her advice to me was "For the sake of the boys, look the other way." I was stunned and felt doubly betrayed.

It turned out that the affair was well-known at his office and that he lived with her and her two children while traveling and that this had been going on for years. His boss later told me that my husband had been passing her off as his wife (the mistress lived in another town).

He returned a week later, but the mask of the contrite man I saw was gone.

Even though he alone was guilty of breaking our marriage vows and dishonoring me, he had become emboldened by the advice of the attorney his mother had hired.

In front of our children, he actually laid out his plan for my destiny.

He was going to move back into our home and drive me insane. He would then have me committed to a mental institution (He had already chosen it!) and then would take possession of all our joint property: house, cars, money, etc., and finally, he would take the boys. I thought even then that the boys were last on his list. I think his hope was that I would die in the institution and he would be rid of me.

When they heard his plans for me, our little boys began to wail, and they pitifully clung to me. My husband's face was like stone; no feeling at all could be found in his eyes. I was already dead to him.

As I stared at him, numb with shock, I thought, *What kind of person does this?*

I instantly began to pray silently, "Dear Lord, I cannot handle this alone. Please help me." Right away, I felt a peace within me that I couldn't explain.

My husband was still not finished with telling me his plans. He told me that if I divorced him, he would turn Kyle and Kirk against me. This was the lowest form of blackmail—teaching our sons to loathe their mother!

That was when I made the biggest mistake of my life. I didn't believe him, but that is exactly what he did.

> Listen, The LORD's arm is not too weak to save you,
> nor is his ear too deaf to hear you call.
> —Isaiah 59:1

He stayed with us for two months and tormented me every moment he could, but the strangest thing happened. Even throughout all of this, not only did he not break me, but I also grew stronger every day. He would upset the kids and tell them outlandish lies about me at the dinner table. The boys would cry so much while I calmly comforted them. I assured them that none of their father's words were true.

Just days before Thanksgiving, I begged my husband to leave because with the holidays approaching, this situation would become unbearable. He agreed and silently left us the next day.

Now, let me confess this here: I am not an emotionally strong woman when I am being unjustly attacked, so I knew the source of my daily strength was my Savior. He was protecting and shielding me from the unreasonable wrath of my husband, his mother, and their poisonous words, and dear Jesus had put me in a position to see His power.

> Fear not, for I am with you; be not dismayed, for I
> am your God. I will strengthen you, yes, I will help
> you. I will uphold you with My righteous right hand.
> —Isaiah 41:101

FIVE

REBUILDING

A month after Kevin left us, the boys and I packed up and moved to Virginia. As I said before, dear friends moved us over the Christmas break, and I will be forever grateful for their friendship and love.

My dear siblings lived in Virginia, so it became a time of deep healing for us.

Soon, after the boys were back in school and doing well, I began a new job. It was interesting work; the office setting was lovely, and I used the work skills that I had recently acquired for it.

Meanwhile, my husband still lived in Alabama with his mistress and her children. He would come for his visitation with the boys once a month for a weekend, and oh, how I dreaded those visits.

Those weekends without them were so lonely as we had only been apart for school time for most of their lives.

I was also filled with anxiety; I feared for their safety and mental health. They always (yes, *always*) returned from these visits both depressed and lethargic.

After the divorce became final, I bought a nice, dependable used car and a small house for us. It had a big yard and was a cozy retreat for us.

Life was finally good, and we were a happy but busy little family.

I had been working hard and enjoying it when I began to feel that life was passing me by and something was missing.

One day, I was watching television when a commercial came on; it advertised a new business in town. It was an introductory service where you could meet interesting people and have confidence in knowing they had been screened before you met them. At this time, I only knew coworkers, the boys' teachers, and family.

This service was unique at the time as it wasn't a dating service as we know it today. The people who joined this service filled out a lengthy, in-depth questionnaire and had their backgrounds checked by law enforcement.

The format worked like this: you went to their office, filled out a twenty-six-page questionnaire, had your photograph taken, and waited to hear from the office.

While you waited at home, you were matched with other people based on the office interview and the questionnaire answers. Then, you would receive several small slips of paper in the mail. Typed on them were only these data points about your match: their name, age, and phone number.

That's it. It was now up to either you or your match to call and make a date.

I did not go into the office to see the photos because I thought that would be too shallow of me. I just wanted to be surprised, and I was!

To my surprise, they were all nice men who treated me well; they were thoughtful, interesting, and kind.

I was careful to assure each person before we went out that they understood I was only interested in a social life and that I no longer believed in romance or love.

My boys actually went on several dates with us, and they loved it. My dates would plan activities around them, so it worked out well for everyone.

My membership was for three months, and by then, I was ready to let it lapse even though the boys and I had gained some nice memories because of the experience.

The last referral I received was from someone who kept calling just as we were heading out the door. By the time he called a third time, my oldest son begged me to pick up the phone and speak with the caller. For some reason I still do not understand, my son was very serious about this, so I promised that if that person called again, I would answer it just for him. (Only many years later would I understand that God was our matchmaker!)

The next time he called, we were once again heading out, and the caller began to leave a message. This time, I picked up and began to chat with him. Right away, I felt comfortable with him and discovered that we really did have a lot in common.

We arranged a date, and when the evening came for him to arrive, I was sweeping my walkway. (I know—it's a Southern thing.)

When I saw Bill for the first time (we had both skipped viewing the dating candidates' photos at the office, but we had described ourselves to each other, so I knew it was him), an incredible thing happened. My heart began to race, and yes, for me, it was love at first sight! (It was something I had never believed in and thought was a myth.)

We both realized in a short time that we were perfectly suited for each other.

He had been married before and had custody of his precious four-year-old son. Whenever we would go on a date with our three boys together, they all got along wonderfully.

We married six months later, and I can truly say that he is still the nicest man I've ever met.

We both feel that God created us for each other and feel so blessed as we continue to love and cherish each other.

God led me to the love of my life, and he is a godly man. I am doubly blessed.

Oh yes, the name of that introductory service was Always, and for us, it is!

Great is his faithfulness, His mercies begin afresh
each morning.

—Lamentations 3:23

DEAN

Technically speaking, my youngest son is actually my stepson,
but because I love him so much, I have always regarded him as "the
son of my heart" since I married his daddy. I never referred to him
by that relationship name or thought of him in that way—even to
this day. He is and will always be my beloved son.

To anyone trying to successfully blend a new family, you are
acutely aware of the possible (and perhaps inevitable) pitfalls you
might encounter along the way. Our challenges began early (as to
be expected, I suppose), beginning with my husband's little boy.

So many people over the years have been curious as to how I met
him, and the way I did was most unusual.

On that day, my boyfriend (we weren't even engaged yet) and
I were taking my sons out for a picnic. After we finished with the
picnic, he asked me if I would like to see his house, and I said sure.
His barely four-year-old son was with his mother for the weekend
and would not be returning home until the next day at 3:00 p.m.

But when we drove into his driveway, there was his son—playing
with some other kids in his neighbor's yard. His mother was nowhere
in sight! As it turns out, Dean's mother had had a car accident and
had brought the boy home and left him. He was so cute; he was
dressed from head to toe like a mini G. I. Joe—even his sneakers
were camo.

I quickly realized that my boyfriend needed to be with his
little boy, so my sons and I drove home. On the drive, I prayed and
told God that if He would allow me to raise that boy, I would do
so for Him. My boys kept asking me why Dean's mother had left
him there when he was so young and had a small cut on his nose

because of the wreck. I had no answers for them as it was beyond my understanding as well.

When Bill called later that night, he told me that his son's mother had not called or come over to check on him.

Of course, as I got to know his son, other problems arose—ones not of his own making but were the results of his birth mother abandoning him when he was very young. After she left his father, she moved in with a man who had an apartment with only one bedroom. So she asked Bill to take custody of their son because there was not a bedroom for him. Of course, Bill readily agreed to this arrangement.

One night before we were married, we were so busy that we missed dinner, and we decided to eat at a McDonald's. Bill took everyone's orders, and because the place was packed (it was Christmas Eve), he told all the boys to stay with me in our booth at the back of the restaurant. We piled into the booth, but his son decided to get out. I said, "Where are you going, honey? Daddy said for us to wait here for him." He became agitated and started yelling, "I want my daddy!" When I would not let him out of the booth because it wasn't safe for him due to the holiday crush, he spat in my face. My boys were shocked! As his saliva was streaming down my face, I realized that this moment was an opportunity to show him love and grace. I wiped off my face and looked at him tenderly (he was so surprised that I did not become angry with him) and spoke these words softly to him: "I love you, honey, and I will keep on loving you until you love me back." As my boys watched in utter amazement, that little boy hugged me and told me he was sorry. It was a turning point in our relationship.

Kindness always helps the wounded and misunderstood. I learned this when one day, I had a doctor appointment, and he could not go with me. I explained the reason why he could not come with me and that he would be staying at his old day care until I came back to pick him up.

All went well that day, but when I came to pick him up, the day-care workers were mystified. "Are you giving him drugs?" they asked, and I wondered at this strange question. It seems that when he was there the last time (before our marriage), he was about to be rejected due to his violent behavior and that this was already the third day care that he went to.

I told them no. I told them that I only loved him unconditionally, and this was the result. They were astounded at his gentleness, his kindness (he helped the other kids who were afraid), and his manners. They said it was like he was a different boy altogether, but, you know, that is the power of love at work.

> God is our refuge and strength, always ready to help
> in times of trouble.
>
> —Psalm 46:1

Life with Bill and our newly blended family was going well. We were adapting, adjusting, and enjoying one another.

However, trouble was on the horizon, and we had no idea what was coming our way. Our idyllic home life was about to be shattered. Without our knowledge, my ex-husband, Kevin, and his mother were working furiously behind the scenes against us. They were attempting to convince my oldest son, Kyle, to leave us and live with his dad in Alabama.

They were so persistent that my eleven-year-old son couldn't stand the pressure they were putting on him, so he relented. The next day, he told me that he wanted to live with his dad. I knew this wasn't true because he was happy where he was and had told Bill and me that he loved Bill.

In the end, though, Kyle left and was never the same again.

On the morning his dad came to pick him up, I ran to the closet and collapsed while sobbing. I thought I would die from the heartache.

Time passed, but in my grief, I knew that I badly needed to fill the hours when my youngest son was in school with a meaningful project.

Baking has always been something I greatly enjoyed, so I decided to create some European-style desserts. Approaching a small local restaurant, I hoped they would feature them on their dessert menu. Upon trying them, they were very pleased and agreed to sell these items from a refrigerated case as whole pieces as well as on the menu as individual slices. The restaurant needed to purchase the case and have it installed, and they told me that they would call me when all was ready for my baked goods. As my spirits were lifted by this happy news, I shared it with my family later that day. They were surprised (as I had not told them of my plans in case they failed) but happy too.

A week after this, we went to New Mexico to visit Bill's dad. When I opened the kitchen door to his dad's house, I was taken aback as there was the cutest ten-year-old girl looking back at me. I knew that Bill had a niece, but we were not expecting to find her there since Bill's dad had lived alone for many years after Bill's mom had passed away. We could plainly see that she was neglected. Her name was Ginger, and I was enchanted by her.

On the long drive back to Virginia, we discussed the possibility of becoming her guardians and having her live with us.

When I called her mother and told her what we were proposing, I barely got the words out of my mouth when her mother blurted out, "Oh, yeah! When are you coming to get her?" I said, "Well, it depends on what your daughter says." Her mother repeated her question. We were astounded!

We returned to New Mexico about a month later and brought her home with us as our two sons fully supported the plan. As a matter of fact, Dean gave up his room and moved in with his brother!

We later learned that Ginger's mother had been taking her to bars for four years in an attempt to give her away. She would sit her atop the bar (like she was a door prize) and wait for someone to take her away.

While one of our sons had been taken away from us by evil people, God, in his infinite compassion, had brought another child into our hearts and home. You cannot replace a child with another, but we felt that she needed what we could willingly and lovingly offer her.

God's ways are miraculous!

By the time we arrived home, the restaurant had called to say that it was ready to begin our business together, but God had other plans. Our sweet little girl was emotionally fragile and needed a great deal of care and attention, so I called them back and explained the situation and that I would have to change my plans. We canceled the business arrangement. I have never regretted that decision because Bill and I felt she was sent to us for a reason.

I have always felt that the ways I met Dean and Ginger were divine appointments. God set them apart for my heart to love, nurture, and honor them.

The funny thing is, our youngest son joked that the restaurant deal would have been my "almost claim to fame" because that small restaurant eventually grew into a large chain in the South!

SIX
TESTING

I was about to face the most challenging trial of my life.

> Nothing of value in God's Kingdom is ever achieved
> quickly or without cost.
>
> —Priscilla Shirer

When Kyle left to live with his dad, I knew in my heart that he would not have a normal life. I knew that Kyle living with his father and being under the constant influence of his damaging and controlling grandmother would be bad for him. As you will see, I was correct about this.

Ten months later, my son was visiting us in Virginia for his Christmas break, and we all had a lovely time. The boys were especially happy to be together again.

At bedtime, I tucked in everyone, and they asked me to read them a Bible story and then sing a song. This was always their prelude to the end of their day. I did both and went downstairs to be with my husband. I wanted to talk to him about the wonderful day we just had and how happy I was that we were a whole family again!

Only a few minutes after I said good night to the boys, our sweet niece ran downstairs to find us. She said, "You better come quick! Something's wrong! Kyle is in tears!"

Finding him still sobbing in his bed, I hugged him and asked him what was wrong.

I will never forget his anguished expression and what he said to me. "Mama, I made a terrible mistake in living with dad. I want to come back and live with you again. Can I?"

While my heart was filled with joy, I had to explain to him that while he could come back to live with us, he would have to go back to Alabama temporarily first. We needed to have the judge sign off on his new place of residence. My son did not want to return because he couldn't face the anger of his dad and grandmother. I then had to tell him that if he didn't go back, his dad could have me arrested for kidnapping. He slumped back in the bed and said dejectedly, "I will just have to go back then." He never mentioned coming to live with us again.

With Ginger comfortable in our home and well established in her school, I knew it was time for us to visit Kyle in Alabama. It would be painful for all of us, but we, especially his brothers, missed him so much.

The weekend of our departure arrived, and as we approached my son's new home, I was stunned. There was my dream house! When my ex-husband and I were planning to build our home years earlier, I wanted a beautiful Victorian-style house with a wraparound porch, but he would have none of it. It was standing before me—right down to the lemon-yellow paint and white gingerbread trim with the white rocking chairs that my ex-mother-in-law had bought for me as a new-home gift. (One weekend before our divorce, when the boys and I were visiting my parents in Virginia, she entered our home and stole everything she had ever given me—furniture, silverware, etc.)

Seeing Kyle was traumatic enough, but this obvious insult only added to my pain. I believe this was intentional—to add to my misery. Our visit with my son was brief, and when we left, everyone in the car was crying.

For the next couple of years, Kevin no longer bothered me about when he could visit Kirk, who was living with us, which I thought was odd. In this same time frame, Bill had decided to change careers and move back to New Mexico. This was a dream he had nurtured for years.

When Kevin came to pick up Kirk for his summer visitation, our "Sold" real-estate sign was in the yard. Both of the boys knew we were moving to New Mexico, so this was not a surprise move.

When Kevin saw that sign, our worst nightmare started to unfold.

I had always allowed Kevin to have the boys for the entire summer vacation because he lived out of state and I wanted to make the visitation go as smoothly as possible for the sake of the boys. Although I phoned them while they were gone, it was hard to catch them at home, and when I did, they both seemed distant. I am certain those phone conversations were closely monitored.

Finally, the morning came when Kirk was to be returned home, and we were all excited. A family friend was also visiting at that time, and she was looking forward to seeing him again.

On the day Kirk was to return home, we were going to start preparing for the new school year (checkups, new clothes, school supplies, etc.). The doorbell rang, and I thought, *How odd. Why is he ringing the bell and not just coming inside?*

When I answered the door, I did not see my son or his dad but two strangers—a man and a woman who looked stern and official.

The woman asked, "Are you Lauren Grant?" I said yes, and she handed me a thick packet and said, "You've been served."

The other person was a detective. They both asked to come in.

I took the packet and asked, "What is this?" The server was silent.

I opened the package and discovered that it was a formal charge against Bill. Although they did not tell me who did this, I knew. Kevin had been too smooth and cooperative. Now, he had both of my children!

I later learned that he and his mother (surprise!) had concocted a hideous story for my younger son to tell the authorities with the purpose of not having to return Kirk to me. Basically, he was doing this to cause me emotional anguish and to not have to pay child support any longer.

They had told Kirk that this heinous story was to be told only to anyone in authority and that this was the only way he could live with his brother again.

My precious Bill was accused (according to the documents) of sexually abusing Kirk and also Dean as well! It also claimed that Kirk told me about the abuse and I threatened to punish him if he told anyone. These abuses were supposed to have taken place when I was out of the house and taking Ginger shopping. The problem with this detail is the timing. She was not living with us at the time this was supposed to have happened. Kevin and his mother were not aware of this when they put their diabolical plan into action.

The fabrication went even further. My young and not very physically strong son was supposed to have removed a metal extension ladder from the basement wall—a ladder that was hanging over his head. Then, he was supposed to have carried it up an inclined walkway to a ten-step stairway to where our front-door landing was. Here, he supposedly placed the ladder on the side of the house and climbed onto the roof. Then he supposedly walked across the roof to look through a skylight and into our master bedroom's dressing area to witness my husband abusing Dean. Can you imagine a ten-year-old pulling this off without making a sound?

The detective asked me if he could do the same thing that my son said he did, and I responded, "You *are not* leaving here until you do!"

He told me to flip on the light switch in the dressing area after he got on the roof and knocked three times. I turned on the light, and when I did, he saw an important flaw in the story my ex and his mother had created. Over the years, the tall pine trees that were around our house had dropped so much sap that it was impossible to see through the skylight.

After he came down, the detective told me that there was no way that a little kid could do what he just did. He said that he had great difficulty getting up there even though he was in great shape!

Then, he took Dean and Ginger to another room to question them. Because both children were questioned without me being present, I have only their version to go on, but both had always been truthful. One thing our youngest told me was that the detective asked him if his dad had ever "played" with him. He said, "Yes, all the time. We play baseball and soccer." When the detective explained what he meant, our innocent son exclaimed, "No! That's sick! My dad would never do that!"

All of this was ludicrous to both the detective and the server, but even though it was nonsensical, it was still emotionally devastating to us. Bill volunteered to take a polygraph test,

and of course, he passed easily. He also had to go to the police station to be interviewed by the detective.

We learned after the fact that this is the number one legal tactic for a noncustodial parent to use when trying to change custody.

The outcome of all of this is that the police dropped the charges against Bill and the judge dismissed the case. When Kevin and Kirk were interrogated by the police (they had to be subpoenaed also), the details kept changing, and they saw the accusations for what they were—a tragic ruse to avoid paying child support.

The age when a child could decide where he would live was seven years old, and Kirk chose to live with his dad so he would be with his brother. I thought this would destroy us, but it did not. Bill and I had called upon the Lord and trusted Him to get us through this terrible ordeal, and He did.

> You love Him even though you have never seen Him. Though you do not see Him now, you trust Him; and you rejoice with a glorious, inexpressible joy. The reward for trusting Him will be the salvation of your souls.
>
> —1 Peter 1:8–9

I realized that I would always carry the deep pain of my life with me, but I needed to press on through it. I refused to allow it to rule me.

Setting aside what I couldn't control and focusing on what I could, I made a difficult but right choice: I chose to be happy despite it all, and with God's help, that is what I did, and that decision made all the difference in the quality of my life.

S E V E N

ENCOUNTERS

Our lives went on. We moved to New Mexico, and Bill started his new career. There, we had two encounters with our Lord that greatly affected our lives.

ENCOUNTER 1

Shortly after our move, on a nice and hot summer day, we decided to go tubing on a nearby river to escape the heat. It seemed like any other summer day; it had a brilliant blue sky and snow-white clouds, but I will remember it for the rest of my life.

Where we went was a very popular place to go tubing, and there were several hundred people on the river that day. We felt completely safe.

The current was gentle, and we floated blissfully down the deep-green river together. At one point, the current became stronger, and the river separated Dean from the rest of us. The current was so powerful that none of us could reach him.

His inner tube became lodged underneath the cluster of roots of an overhanging tree and was trapped there! He was in danger of drowning now. When I saw what was happening, my first reaction was to scream his name, and then I begged God to save him.

Within seconds of my prayer, we saw a large man running toward our son. He pulled him out from under the roots that held him fast. As we watched in amazement, the man gently carried Dean and gave him to his dad and said that Dean had a tremendous will to live. The man then went away, and we never saw him again.

When we spoke to others that day, no one seemed to have noticed the man before or after he brought Dean to his dad! Only our family saw him!

We have always felt that he was no mortal man but, in fact, was an angel of the Lord!

Our mighty and compassionate Lord hears our prayers, and He certainly did that day.

ENCOUNTER 2

Several years later, one night, the unexpected happened. When we returned from my birthday dinner, Bill checked our phone messages while I was in another room. He came to get me and said, "You are not going to believe this. Go! Listen to the phone message."

It was a message from Kyle; he said that he wanted to come for a visit! How amazing!

I immediately called him back and asked him for details. He said he would call back the next day with details of the date, flight, etc.

The call never came.

I finally called him, and he quietly told me that Kevin had changed his mind and that the trip was not going to happen after all. I softly told him how disappointed we were and that we loved him very much regardless.

When I hung up the phone, I was furious—not at Kevin or Kyle but at God! I shouted to Him, "Why is this happening to me? I have never stopped loving and caring about my sons, and I have been a good mother to them!"

Then a remarkable thing took place.

At the instant those words left my mouth, I "heard" His voice say, "Kirk has to come first because he has to heal first."

My spirit was instantly calmed and began to wait on the Lord.

Exactly one year later, Kirk called us; he wanted to come for a visit, but first, he wanted to speak to Bill. He begged for Bill's forgiveness for the lies he told, and Bill forgave him. He knew that Kirk was just an innocent pawn in the evil scheme originated by his father and grandmother.

A year after that conversation, Kyle came for a visit.

Both visits were odd because they shared a common thread. They seemed to be only interested in learning about my life but not me as a person. I now feel that they were sent by their father to check up on me as he was always curious about me before and after we were divorced. I still do not understand him or how he thinks.

Many more years passed with no word from either son.

While they were silent as those years passed by, a profound change was happening to me.

> "My thoughts are nothing like your thoughts," says the LORD. "And my ways are far beyond anything you could imagine. For just as the heavens are higher than the earth, so my ways are higher than your ways and my thoughts are higher than your thoughts."
> —Isaiah 55:8–9

God used those years to refine me as a believer. I became patient and trusted Him like never before, and my growth as a Christian became stronger as my faith deepened.

Many have asked me over the years how I managed to go on when many would not have been able to survive all this sadness.

This is my answer: I had to learn that when suffering happened in my life, the scriptures reveal that God can bring good out of evil when I surrender to Him with gratitude. I have been fortunate enough to witness this truth in my everyday life countless times. I thank Him for all things seen and unseen, spoken and unspoken.

EIGHT
A FALSE BEGINNING

After many years of not hearing from Kyle, he contacted me and said he was moving to Albuquerque. He told me he wanted to get to know me better and have a relationship with me. I was thrilled, of course, but it turned out to only be a dream. He was merely interested in having a free place to stay with meals provided and no responsibility.

He had told me that his girlfriend, Jennifer, was finishing up her college degree here in Albuquerque. She would be living in a dorm for a while, and then they would move into an apartment together. I wasn't thrilled about them living together in an apartment without being married, but it was not my decision.

They were both flying into Albuquerque on the same day, and their flights were scheduled to arrive at about the same time. Jennifer's flight arrived first as Kyle's flight was delayed many times due to weather and actually arrived the following day. Since we didn't know this at the time, we patiently waited for Kyle at the airport for several hours. This gave us the opportunity to learn more about Jennifer. She was (and still is) a loving, caring, bright, and honest woman, and we bonded right away.

When my son finally got into town the following day, everyone breathed easier, and it was a joy to see him again.

Soon, Jennifer was attending classes and living in her dorm, while Kyle was staying with us.

We kept waiting for him to accept some responsibility or take initiative by offering to help with chores, contribute financially for groceries—something! He only wanted to read and sleep the days away. Finally, I asked about his plans for the future and discovered he had not even thought about it!

I assisted him with setting up a bank account and drove him to job interviews since he did not have a car. When he needed to get a drug test to complete a job application, he kept putting it off. I had endured enough of this and finally forced him to go take the test. He passed easily and was hired by IBM.

He seemed to have no ambition. We have since learned that his father didn't expect him to excel or even have goals, and this was the result.

Eventually, Kyle and Jennifer moved into an apartment together. While my son and I did have a sort of rapport, I was only a means to an end for him. It was sad as he finally had the chance he said he had been waiting for—the chance to reconnect with us—but he squandered it.

When Jennifer unexpectedly became pregnant, we were surprised but still happy as this was our first grandchild.

Their relationship was in turmoil, however, and Kyle wanted her to terminate the pregnancy! We offered to raise the baby as an alternative to abortion, but I didn't get the opportunity to discuss it with Jennifer because by this time, she had left him and moved in with her parents so that the baby could have a peaceful environment. Although her move was difficult for us, she was wise to do so.

In hindsight, we were grateful that they did not get married because it would have certainly ended in a nasty divorce.

Baby Timothy was born very early and had many serious health issues. In fact, he nearly died several times. Thankfully, he survived and has grown up to be a fine, intelligent young man.

Kyle went to the hospital for the birth of his son. He was so angry, rude, and unreasonable that he was asked to leave the hospital. In the midst of all of this, we only knew of the birth and the health issues. We knew nothing of the emotional fireworks Kyle had heaped on everyone.

Out of the blue, I got a phone call from Kyle. He demanded that I never speak to Timothy about him. I had no idea what he meant, so I tried to get him to clarify what he was telling me. He would not, and he only repeated his demand. I told him that of course, I would tell Timothy about his dad (unaware of what was really going on). Since I did not agree with his demand, he told me, "You have made your decision. You will not hear from me or see me ever again." He then hung up the phone.

He was true to his word. There had been no contact with him all these years despite us trying to reach out to him. He seemed lost to us.

Jennifer has evolved into a wonderful mother and an exceptional person in her own right. Over the years, we have been in touch and have visited many times. Bill and I were there for Timothy's christening, his confirmation in the Lutheran Church, and his college graduation. (More about this will be discussed later in the book.)

NINE

DOUBLE BLESSINGS

One day, I decided to take a leap of faith and write Kyle and Kirk a note. By now, they were both in their forties, and I wrote that I would like to have a place in their lives and prayed they were well and happy. I signed it with "All my love forever, Mom."

I did not hear from Kyle as a result of this note.

A week later, I got an email from Kirk. It was a sweet message that told me that he was now married and that when he and his adorable wife, Mary, read my note together, she reminded him that he really did not know what kind of person I was because his memories of me had been erased over time.

We now keep in touch regularly, and those phone calls and emails are glorious!

Twenty-three years since the last time we saw each other, Bill and I drove to their home in Alabama. When we stopped in front of their house, my husband stayed behind a little bit, and my darling daughter-in-law did the same.

Kirk and I ran to each other and hugged tightly and long. We were both weeping, and he kept repeating, "I'm so glad you are here." My eyes still fill with tears whenever I recall that miraculous experience. Mother and son were together at last.

Even now, many years later, our relationship is still a close one; our feelings for each other have not changed at all. When we chat, no subject is off-limits, and he knows I will always be truthful with him.

I tell his precious wife often that she is our angel because God used her to reunite us all, and we will forever be grateful to her. She is such a delight, and we love her dearly.

We serve such a powerful God!

Even though I had not seen or heard from Kyle, I learned some things about his life, and they were most discouraging. I don't know why I am surprised by the outcome of his life, considering the relationship that he had with his dad and grandmother.

He lives with his dad, does not own a car, will not work, and is addicted to video gaming. His dad is in good health, so he doesn't need a live-in caretaker, but my son decided to assume this role.

This is particularly tragic because as a child, he was kind, loving, and helpful to others. He was very intelligent and had the potential to lead a productive life. Now, I understand that he is a cynical person and an atheist. My heart aches for him, and I pray daily for him.

TEN

GRACE

When I was fifty years old, I received word that my mother was very ill with cancer. She had smoked four packs of cigarettes daily for forty years, so I wasn't surprised by this unfortunate news. I also heard that she was asking to see me. Knowing that this could very well be the last time we would see each other, I could not refuse her.

> My heart has heard you say, "Come and talk with me" and my heart responds LORD I am coming.
> —Psalm 8:27

Although she had a toxic personality, she was still my mama. So I gathered up my courage and flew to Arizona to be with her. This trip was quite a difficult decision for me because I had been estranged from her for many years. On the flight to Phoenix, I asked Jesus to forgive me for not forgiving Mama for the abuse that I had experienced from her. As I did so, I felt an easing in my heart.

She met me at the airport, and our greeting was strained. Then, we began the two-hour drive to her home in Sedona. Once we were in the car and well on our way, she began to rant and shout; on and on came the ugly words.

I said nothing but continued to look out the car window and take in the desert view. Silently I began praying for God to send me the right words to soothe and comfort her. When she finally stopped yelling, I turned to her and said in a soft, tranquil voice, "Mama, it doesn't matter what you say or do. I will always love you."

She quickly pulled over at the side of the road and cut off the engine. I really did not know what to expect from her. Would she hurt me again—physically or emotionally—like so many other times before when we were alone?

Sobbing now, she took me in her arms, and I told her that I forgave her for the abuse that she poured on me while I was growing up.

Here is an interesting twist to this scene. She did not ask for my forgiveness or admit her abuse. This is what came from her mouth next: "If I did those things, then you probably deserved it." Although I was stunned by those words and her belligerent attitude, I chose to let them go as I now realized how broken she was inside. She did not have the capacity to admit her wrongdoing—much less to feel remorse.

It was a breakthrough in our relationship, though, and God enabled us to enjoy a warm mother-daughter weekend together in spite of her harsh words.

Right before we were to leave for the airport for my return flight home, she had an unusual request for me: she asked if I could sing "The Sound of Music" (her favorite song) so she could record it and listen to it after I left her.

I thought this was odd, but of course, I agreed to sing it for her. A few months later, I learned the reason. She asked her hospice nurse to play that recording as she lay dying. God truly works in mysterious ways and in ways we cannot agree with or fully understand.

I am so grateful that I was able to give Mama some comfort in her greatest time of need.

His loving grace has equipped me with a voice that draws others out of the darkness and into His marvelous light when I sing His praises.

All praise to God, Father to our Lord Jesus Christ. God is our merciful Father and the source of all comfort. He comforts us in all our troubles so that we can comfort others.

—2 Corinthians 1:3–4

As my life unfolded, the Lord gave me the endurance and patience I needed to move forward in my journey of faith.

Please know this truth: sometimes life gets so hard that it hurts to take a breath, but we are not godforsaken but children of the king.

For the word of the LORD holds true, and we can trust everything he does. He loves whatever is just and good, the unfailing love of the LORD fills the earth.

—Psalm 33:4–5

ELEVEN

TRAVELING ON

Although some days I felt far away from Him, I chose to keep on going, not understanding but trusting Him with my life regardless. He protected me from challenges that He knew I was not prepared to handle well.

> Faith is acting like it is so.
> Even when it is not so.
> In order that it might be so.
> Simply because God said so.
>
> —Dr. Tony Evans

My God also gave me His divine protection as I encountered a series of accidents.

Although it is not an accident, the following is an example of God's protection at work.

My husband and I were driving home at night. We had attended our grandson's christening and got a late start for our trip home. I was concerned about all the nocturnal wildlife we would be encountering since many only feel safe coming out at night.

I began to pray for God to please hold the animals on the side of the road until we passed them so they would not get hurt and would not hurt us as well. Time after time, I saw large groups of deer gathered together, waiting for our car to pass. When I looked back, I saw them casually walking across the road. What a miracle!

ACCIDENT 1

While driving home from work one day during rush hour, I saw some movement to my right. To my astonishment, a huge deer (the largest that I had ever seen—what antlers it had!) jumped a barbed-wire fence and leaped onto my car's hood, shattering the windshield. Fortunately, I had the presence of mind to calmly and slowly steer the car into the left-hand lane and safely pull into a drugstore's parking lot.

Bill was working a late shift and could not leave work to get me. So I called a good friend, and he came to take me home. When he arrived, he gave me a warm hug and then took a good look at the car. He was stunned by how much damage there was. I was so shaken by the event that I had not really looked at it. I also was stunned: the car was totaled, but I was completely uninjured! Not even a scratch!

When my husband finally got off work, he went to get the car and drive it home. The next morning, he was going to drive it to our insurance agent to get an estimate on the damages. When he looked closer at the damage done to the car in the daylight, he saw that the damage was far more serious than we realized. He couldn't believe that he had been able to drive it home. He mentioned that if the deer had hit only six inches closer to me, I probably would have been seriously injured or even killed.

ACCIDENT 2

While dusting the chandelier in our dining room, I stepped away from it to look at something else. At this time, it came crashing down onto our glass dining-room table, missing my head by only a few inches! Because of its weight and its pointed bottom feature, had it struck me, I feel certain that it might have seriously injured or even killed me. But once again, my precious Lord allowed me to walk away unharmed.

> Every word of God is pure; He is a shield to those
> who put their trust in Him.
>
> —Proverbs 30:5

I began to ask God for strength and guidance for only that one day, and He has blessed me abundantly for it. Seeing a pattern developing in my spirit, asking only for today and not for tomorrow, in trust He lead me out of the wilderness of my heart.

Now, I began to thrive and search for ways to honor and please God. Years passed as I was being filled with grace, compassion, and encouragement for myself and others.

Soon, I became aware of the glorious healing power of Jesus— first from the magnificence of the natural world and then His working through the lives of other Christians who were helping me.

Feeling empowered with authentic joy and hope for a continued meaningful life, I too began to reach out to help others.

> And now, just as you accepted Christ Jesus as your
> LORD, you must continue to follow Him. Let your
> roots grow down into Him. Then your faith will
> grow strong in the truth you were taught and you
> will overflow with thankfulness.
>
> —1 Colossians 2:6

My precious husband is going through a life-changing battle, and because I love him so, I am feeling his pain also. I have surrendered his battle to Almighty God and feel at peace. This will be a long and terrible ordeal, but this I do know: We will come out of this heart-wrenching testing because God has allowed it in our lives for a reason.

I believe His purpose is to show His glory through our lives, which are committed to Him and to each other. We both understand that without great and sometimes very painful trials, we will not have a great testimony. God is in control of the universe and certainly our lives. If our hearts and minds are open to Him, He will purify us, and our lives will reflect this.

> For those who know Your name trust in You, for You, O Lord, do not abandon those who search for You.
>
> —Psalm 9:10

T W E L V E

FOUND

Almost seventy-seven years old now, I am the happiest in my life and have reached a time of abundance. This feeling is not due to my own efforts but my heavenly Father at work in me. How far I have come.

Each day is a blessing, and I thank Him as soon as I open my eyes each morning. I am eager to travel on the path He has planned for me. His divine plans may be filled with moments of joy, challenge, discovery, or sorrow, but I know my Savior will be holding my hand as I experience it all with Him. I trust Him with all my life.

Choosing to live a simple way, listening for God's voice, and following Him have made all the difference for me in achieving my whole and contented life.

> Let the morning bring me word of Your unfailing
> love for I have put my trust in You. Show me the
> way I should go, for to You I have entrusted my life.
> —Psalm 143:8

A joyous time was when our oldest grandson, Timothy, graduated from college in Arizona. Bill and I, as well as his mom's family, attended it. Imagine my feelings when I learned that Kyle was coming! When we saw each other, we tightly embraced, and I told him how much I loved him (we had not seen each other since before Timothy's birth). He smiled and said, "I know."

I uplifted my son to the Father years ago, and I am now at peace after having seen him. Thank You, Lord, for this experience.

All through my life, I have experienced the awesome power of God in it. I finally understood that to depend on Him—to lean on Him—was not a sign of weakness but of power—His power.

> Yet I still belong to you; You hold my right hand.
> You guide me with your counsel, leading me to a
> glorious destiny. Whom have I in heaven but You?
> I desire You more than anything on earth. My
> health may fail, and my spirit may grow weak, but
> God remains the strength of my heart, He is mine
> forever.
>
> —Psalm 73:23–26

THIRTEEN

MY SIBLINGS

You may be wondering what became of my siblings when they arrived at adulthood.

Wilson, the youngest of the family, died unexpectedly as a result of a horrific motorcycle crash. As you can imagine, our lives were forever altered as a family on that day.

Beth died a few years ago in Alaska where she had spent many years of her life living in the wild—without the benefits of electricity or running water. This was her choice because she wanted to immerse herself in the rugged beauty of her adopted state.

I believe those years took a tremendous toll on her health. The cause of her death is still unknown.

Then came the loss of Walter, Warren's identical twin brother. He tragically passed from a lifetime of drug addiction.

Thankfully, Warren is still with us. As a young man, he educated himself well, worked hard, and accomplished much in his life. He blesses others by helping the many people who cross his path.

His life is now dedicated to God's service. He honors his family and friends and is a credit to our family in every way.

FOURTEEN

CHILDREN

Our children are all adults now; they have found their way in the world, and several have children of their own.

Kyle is a single dad and lives in Alabama with his father. Kyle has an exceptionally fine son who lives in New Mexico.

Kirk also lives in Alabama—one hour away from his brother—and is blissfully married to our precious Mary.

Our niece, Ginger, lives in New Mexico and is a dedicated and loving mom to two sweet and special daughters and a gifted son. Ginger is and will always be a joy to us.

Dean lives in New Mexico as well, and he is happily married. He and his wife are proud parents of two bright and athletic sons.

The Lord has blessed everyone in our family greatly and in unique ways.

Filled with wonder and grace, I am very thankful to be a part of it all as our lives continue to be the adventure that God planned for us.

FIFTEEN

MOMENTS OF JOY

GOD PREPARING MY HEART FOR A LIFELONG JOURNEY

God has used many milestones to direct me to Him throughout my life. Here are a few of them.

When I was in my twenties, my husband and I, along with two other couples, decided to go on a fishing weekend in a nearby small coastal town. While the guys went fishing one morning, we girls planned to do some shopping instead. My friend Cindy was driving. Ellen was in the passenger seat, and I was in the back seat.

We were happily chatting away and looking at the scenery when I spotted an unusual sight. It was an old man who was fully dressed in blue overalls and a long-sleeved shirt. He was lying very still on his back in the dirt backyard behind a house. It was a sweltering day, so I knew right away that he wasn't taking a nap.

I alerted the girls to what I had seen and told them, "We need to go over there and check this out. He might be hurt." Immediately my friends told me that we were not getting involved. They said that it wasn't safe for us and he would be fine.

My friends were not hard-hearted, but they were frightened and being cautious. I understood that, but at that moment, an overpowering and urgent feeling came over me, and I began yelling, "Turn around! Turn around!" They both shouted back, "OK! OK! Calm down!" Cindy quickly turned the car around, and we pulled into the old man's backyard as there was no driveway.

He was still lying there! When the car came to a stop, I jumped out and ran to him. He was unconscious but still breathing. But I couldn't wake him. I ran to the back door of the house and knocked many times. Since I couldn't get a response, I finally pounded on the door. A woman's angry voice yelled through the closed door, "What do you want?" I told her about the man, and she jerked the door open, took one look at him, and ran past me to go to him.

By this time, someone else was standing in the doorway, and the woman shouted at her to call an ambulance.

An ambulance and the police arrived quickly. One of the ambulance attendants told us that if we had not found him when we did, he probably would not have survived as he was in pretty bad condition.

It seems that he was housebound but managed to get outdoors without anyone noticing.

His family was now very grateful for our help, and the police kept asking me for my name. I asked why they wanted to know. An officer told me that they were going to publish a police report in their local newspaper and the community wanted to thank me. I did not give my name because it didn't seem right for me to be singled out like that. I was doing what the Holy Spirit wanted me to do. We left without giving my name to them, and my heart was at peace once more.

When I was in my thirties, I was baptized on the same evening as our precious niece, Ginger, and Kirk. What a glorious, exhilarating evening! I really did feel that all my sins had been washed away by those healing and redemptive waters. My relationship with Jesus had been renewed.

When I was in my sixties, two incredible opportunities presented themselves that would allow the Lord to work in my life.

The first was quite unexpected. One Sunday morning, as I was taking my seat next to my husband, I noticed one chair, a basin, and a pitcher of water on the stage and thought, *That is odd.*

Our minister began his sermon with a startling announcement: "Someone in this sanctuary will come forward, walk onto the stage, and allow me to wash their feet. I do not know who it will be."

Inwardly I chuckled and said to myself, "Good luck with that! Who is going to sign up for this?"

To my utter amazement, that person was me! I found myself standing up and walking onto the stage. Here is the surreal thing: I was completely calm, filled with peace, humble, and not embarrassed at all. It felt like the most natural thing in the world to be doing this (especially since it was televised as well) because it was God's plan and He was doing the leading at this time.

Many people have asked me over the years if our minister and I planned this, and the answer is no. It was a God moment, and He was showing up in my life yet again.

Washing someone's feet is an act of Christian love, humility, and service. It signifies forgiveness and bearing with that person their daily problems. It emphasizes that we care for each other as Jesus cares for us.

The other episode was when I felt compelled to go on a Walk to Emmaus weekend.

When I shared this with two of my dearest friends, they were very happy for me. One of them told us that she had been praying for two years for this to happen. I had no idea.

The Walk to Emmaus is a Christian experience of faith renewal—a three-day course in Christianity. You meet with a large body of fellow pilgrims (groups are separated by gender) to learn and share your faith in a new way as God's grace and love are revealed that weekend to us through other believers.

To say that it was a powerful and transformational experience would be an understatement. It was truly life-changing—thrilling, fulfilling, and supportive. I was filled with joy, gratitude, and communion with my Lord as He inspired me to become his disciple wherever I went.

Last but not least was the blessing of Deeper Journey when I was in my early seventies. It helped me to delve deeper into God's Word and lean in closer to Jesus and trust Him more with every prayer.

It was helpful, encouraging, and insightful, and it was always presented in a way that reflected God's deep and abiding love for me. It was the final piece of the puzzle that unlocked my life. I was now a healed and restored woman of God.

SIXTEEN

How God Turned My Life Around

To begin His work in me, He completely cleansed away the traumas of my childhood and early marriage. He accomplished this by using Deeper Journey, which is an in-depth, two-year Bible study led by our women's pastor. He then began to mold my life anew for His purposes. As I experienced His love, I began to reflect it.

Galatians 5:22–23 reveals to us the fruits of the Spirit, and they are love, joy, peace, patience, kindness, goodness, faithfulness, gentleness, and self-control.

When we model these virtues in our daily lives, unbelievers as well as fellow believers will take notice. You have become different by choice, and this change will inspire them to desire what you now have—a better life. Your sole purpose is to glorify Him. It is why God created us—to love Him and others, to worship Him, and to help grow His church.

I think of my grace-filled life as a faucet. I leave the tap open, and opportunities to show His love stream from it. God allows them to flow through me so I can honor Him and reflect His glory. Every believer has the opportunity to serve God in some kind of ministry. It is helpful to know that not everyone has the same role, but we all have the same calling to use our gifts in God's service.

The ways to serve are only limited by our imagination. When I began to think about what I wanted to do, I was mystified, so I prayed and asked God to show me what He wanted me to do. Very shortly, He filled my mind with ideas that I normally would not have considered! Here's the thing: If you are truly anxious to become God's servant, He will respond, so be ready for His answer! (This is the way He uses me, but He may use a different method for someone else.)

> Each of you should use whatever gift you have received to serve others, as faithful stewards of God's grace in its various forms.
>
> —1 Peter 4:10

Here are some of the ways I serve Him:

—writing anonymous notes of encouragement to uplift others;

—seeding ministry—I write scripture on a small piece of paper, fold it in half, and insert it into a library book so it can be discovered by a reader;

—volunteering at a food pantry in my town. I do this to help these dear people grocery-shop, and sharing God's love blesses me also;

—baking/delivering goodies to friends and family when they are not expecting it;

—sing in the choir. I have been doing this since I was thirteen years old, so this was an easy one;

—daily devotion;

—participating in the women's Good Friday service. It is held in my church's campus at a beautiful rose garden with a stream nearby. I lead the hymns sung by the group and open and close the service with a solo. All singing is a cappella, so the effect is enchanting and prepares our hearts for Easter. A dear friend hands out a fresh rose to each woman attending;

—writing Monday-morning prayer thoughts. This is a team effort by many talented writers in our church. They create a different devotion and post it online every Monday. The format is a scripture, a message, and then a closing prayer. This cheers, inspires, and blesses each reader. I know when I read the ones from the other ladies, my heart and mind are soothed and encouraged. I eagerly await Monday mornings now; and

—serving during Communion.

Speaking of using our gifts, do you know which ones you can use to further the mission of Jesus?

Here are some ways that I would like to share. Several of my friends have used these opportunities in their walks with God.

—Hospitality. I have a sweet friend who is brilliant in the art of bringing women of all backgrounds and ages together to meet, brainstorm, and enjoy fellowship. The food is always delicious, and the setting is very attractive—a win-win for everyone.

—One of my dear friends makes dresses for little girls in Africa.

—I have another friend who has a heart for missionary work and travels to other countries to bring the Word of God to those who would not normally have learned about Jesus.

—A gifted baker by trade, another friend bakes stunning cookies and volunteers in my church's cafe.

—Another precious friend became a minister. She did not expect this turn of events in her life, but that's how He works. When you offer up your life to serve God, He does some pretty amazing things.

—One of my dearest friends quietly uses her life as a living testimony for Christ by helping as many people as she can and living humbly.

What will your walk with God look like?

A beautiful life of service is awaiting you; God wants you to look inward and listen to Him so He can showcase your talents and you can serve Him with all your heart, body, mind, and soul.

SEVENTEEN

A FEW MONDAY-MORNING PRAYER THOUGHTS

PRAYER THOUGHT 1

Let's See What Love Can Do

> Give thanks to the LORD, for He is good! His
> faithful love endures forever.
>
> —Psalm 8:1–2

Is today the day you have been dreading—that impossible work deadline, the medical-test results, or the arrival of a difficult family member coming for a visit?

Although at the time, we often cannot see God's loving involvement in our lives, He is there, working in the background for our benefit. Why? Because He loves us more than we can fathom.

> With You is the fountain of life, in your light we
> see light.
>
> —Psalm 36:9

> And we know that God causes everything to work
> together for the good of those who love God and are
> called according to His purpose for them.
>
> —Romans 8:28

When I read and meditate on these scripture verses, I am uplifted again and can face the hard things of life with hope, gratitude, and renewed purpose.

Our loving Father provides a fresh outlook for our lives and peaceful rest for our souls despite the overwhelming problems we face each day.

Trust Him and call on Him. He will answer.

Magnificent Lord,

> I place my heartache and confusion at Your feet and
> humbly accept Your love, healing, and mercy. Amen

PRAYER THOUGHT 2

Rest Now?

> Come to me, all of you who are weary and carry
> heavy burdens, and I will give you rest.
>
> —Matthew 11:28

Summer is perhaps the busiest season of the year for American families—sleepovers, camping, sporting events, water parks, travel, etc.

While we enjoy all these activities, sometimes it seems that we "run ourselves ragged" (an old Southern expression that means "to wear ourselves out"!). Now I must admit here that I am guilty of this too. The weather is gorgeous, and the kids are finally out for summer vacation. Bring on the water wings, squirt guns, snacks, and lack of schedules! Yippee!

But eventually, our busyness catches up with us and forces us to slow down because we have exhausted ourselves having all that fun!

Take naps when you can, eat healthy, and above all, remember the Lord. It is He who made this possible for you and your family.

Remember Him because only Jesus can give us true and deep rest—for our bodies, minds, and hearts. Take a moment to thank Him for all His blessings.

What do I mean by "deep rest"? It is when we completely trust the sovereignty of God. We lean into His Holy Spirit even when we are spent and our lives are "filled to the brim."

We experience this when we spend time in His presence, praying and reflecting on His Word. Be still, silent, and present and allow Him to work in our lives.

Compassionate Lord,

Your love knows no bounds, and we are deeply grateful for each moment. We crave your deep rest, and as we partake of it, we are blessed many times over.

In Your guiding name,
Amen

PRAYER THOUGHT 3

The Real Control

We make our plans, but the LORD determines our steps.

—Proverbs 16:9

There are moments in our lives when we think (in error) that we have our lives all figured out, but no matter how carefully we mapped out our plans, God's plans are often quite different from ours. For one thing, His plans are bigger than ours. Sometimes He places obstacles in our path (to get our attention) that we would have never imagined we would encounter. But take heart as every day is an opportunity to test out our obedience to Him. We must be obedient as it is the only way to trust, grow, and understand what God has called us to do with our precious time here on this beautiful planet He created for us. How do we do this?

Step one: Release control of our plans (and this is difficult for many of us) and ask God what His plans are for us.

I know this step firsthand as it seems to be a recurring theme in my life. I tend to make a plan and then blast off to "get it done." Most of the time, I am successful with this approach. This is not always a good thing because if I can handle it all by myself, then why would I need God?

Sweet sisters, let me just tell you that we *all* need Him and in more ways than we can imagine!

Step two: Be thankful for God's presence in our lives and realize that He loves us completely, deeply, and without reservation.

Step three: Humble ourselves before our Creator's awesome power and unlimited grace.

When I take these three steps, amazing things begin to happen. I feel at peace; my mind becomes clear, and I feel God's love as never before. His path will always be the right one to take, but because I am weak, I forget this.

I have come to know that the seeds of kindness, compassion, grace, and love that I am planting now will one day grow into a beautiful, strong tree. Others will find shelter under this tree too from the storms of life they will encounter. Why? Because those seeds were born of God's plan for us.

Dearest Lord, my deepest desire is to obey You in all areas of my life and to allow my decisions to become those directed by Your commands. Thank You for showing me the way to do this.

Amen

PRAYER THOUGHT 4

True Value

And the very hairs of your head are all numbered. Don't be afraid, you are worth more than many sparrows.

—Luke 12:7

When our hairs are numbered, we are carefully watched over; this reflects the boundless love God has for us.

Because God created each of us, He knows everything about us; nothing is hidden from Him.

He loves us deeper than anyone ever could, and He made us what we are.

Our true value comes only from Him—not our professions, bank accounts, social standings, or physical appearances.

This morning, during my daily devotion, I came upon this scripture:

Be strong and courageous, do not be afraid, do not be discouraged, for the LORD your God will be with you wherever you go.

—Joshua 1:9

As I read it, I began to sob as it brought a recent memory to mind.

On Good Friday, my brother had a terrible car crash, yet he amazingly survived. He lives on a mountain, and while driving home from church, he fell asleep at the wheel while going sixty-five miles per hour. He awoke as his car flew off the side of the mountain and plunged headfirst into a stone ravine. The state patrol said it was an "unsurvivable accident," and yet his only injuries were two broken ribs, two broken fingers, and some minor internal injuries. On Easter Sunday, he was recovering at his home.

Even though those words were spoken to Joshua as he was about to enter the "Promised Land," it remains true today.

God will always be with us wherever we go—even into a stone ravine.

Gracious, loving Father,

My heart sings with joy as I celebrate your unconditional promises of protection, faithfulness, grace, and love.

Amen

PRAYER THOUGHT 5

Change the Recipe

For the LORD grants wisdom! From His mouth comes knowledge and understanding.
—Proverbs 2:6

For years, I have been attending a delightful and spirit-nourishing Bible study in the home of the teacher. The studies are excellent, and the fellowship is loving,

One time per month, each woman provides brunch for the group. Their culinary offerings are tasty and attractive.

I have so many recipes that the sheer volume is staggering. It is a vast sixty-year collection. To say that I am a recipe collector is an understatement!

Yet with all these recipes, I still like to try something new.

When it is my turn to cook for the group, I create my dishes ahead of time—kind of like a dress rehearsal—and my sweet husband is the chief taster.

I once found what I thought was the perfect breakfast casserole, but after we tasted it, we found that a certain something was missing. I changed a few ingredients, and the result was delicious.

This simple discovery made me begin to think about how intentional changes could make all the difference in our lives too.

When we try to solve our own problems without asking for God's help, we will never get the results we desire. But when we do ask for His guidance, we become capable of changing not only what is inside of us but also how we respond to our problems.

That's the way God works in our daily lives. Whenever our actions or thinking needs changing, He leads us to "change the recipe" to get us back on track to living for Him.

Dear Lord,

Thank You for showing us Your ways so our lives may honor You.

Amen

PRAYER THOUGHT 6

One of Your Own

So be happy when you are insulted for being a Christian, for then the glorious Spirit of God rests upon you.

—1 Peter 4:14

We all know that suffering is part of the human experience because we live in a broken world.

How I wish I had known that when I was a teenager, having to deal with not only the normal teen challenges but also living with my fractured family as well.

When I was sixteen years old, my mother sought family counseling with our minister regarding handling problems with raising my rowdy twin brothers. They were really quite a handful! When the minister did not give her the answers she wanted, she decided our entire family would leave the church. They never returned.

When she told me what he said, I thought his advice seemed sound and logical, but I was not about to say that to my volatile mother. What a temper she had!

The following Sunday, I attended church alone, but when I returned home, she was waiting for me and began to criticize and insult me and call me hurtful names because I went without them.

While the words stung, somehow I hung on and kept attending church. Several months later, there came a change in her, though. I began to teach a Sunday School class for four-year-olds. When she learned this, she gave up on hounding me.

In the book of Amos, we learn how the prophet was persecuted for honoring God. Prophets were constantly mocked and persecuted because of their faith. Now when I think of those memories of my sixteen-year-old self, I feel that I was in good company.

If this is an issue for you right now, here is an encouraging scripture for you.

> But it is no shame to suffer for the privilege of being called by His name.
>
> —1 Peter 4:16

Merciful Lord,

Thank You for the honor of being one of Your own and to serve You. Even though life is sometimes heartbreaking, I am comforted to know that You never let go of my right hand. You love me deeply and without reservation for all eternity.

In Your loving name,
Amen

PRAYER THOUGHT 7

Tears in a Bottle

You keep track of all my sorrows. You have collected all my tears in Your bottle. You have recorded each one in Your book.

—Psalm 56:8

When I turn on the news and learn about the fresh misery, pain, and chaos being unleashed upon the world, my heart aches—literally.

As I begin to pray for the people and situations I witnessed on that broadcast, I also realize that the psalmist was right. Knowing that my tears (and those from around the globe) are in God's bottle calms and comforts me.

One day, there will be no more pain, suffering, or mourning. While this seems like an impossible thing, we have His assurance of this reality. It is one of our Lord's many promises to us.

A soothing thought that is helpful is that during our earthly struggle, God never gives up on us. His grace is greater than any problem we might have to face. His love endures forever and triumphs over everything in our earthly existence.

When Jesus died on the cross and arose from His tomb, He revealed God's love for us.

So we don't look at the troubles we can see now.
Rather, we fix our gaze on things that cannot be

seen. For the things, we see now will soon be gone, but the things we cannot see will last forever.

—2 Corinthians 4:18

So go ahead and weep, dear ones, for every tear you shed is preparing you for His kingdom that is awaiting you.

Loving Lord,

Our hearts echo with the cries of the agonized and fearful, but one day, they will be filled with joy.

In Your glorious name,
Amen

EIGHTEEN
THE FARM YEARS

TALE 1: FISH DAY

One day, my sister, my three brothers, and I awoke to an unnaturally quiet morning; the absence of animal sounds (even birds chirping) was eerie.

We all bounded into the kitchen where Mama told us what had happened.

"During the night, a heavy rainstorm came and lasted all through the night." That's all she said. Then, she grinned widely and told us to open the back door.

When we did, we were shocked and stared with our mouths agape. There were fish everywhere! They covered our porch, our yard, and even our car. And that smell—ugh!

Mama soon solved the mystery and told us that so much rain had fallen in a short period that our neighbor's lake had spilled over its banks and the fish had swum out!

Of course, they were dead by now, so the entire family (except for Daddy, who was already at work at the time) had to go outside, pick them up, and dispose of them. Talk about awful work! The whole time, my twin brothers were laughing about the weird situation. Soon, we were all laughing, but then the twins began throwing the fish at the rest of us. My siblings were always fun and could usually find some humor in an otherwise disgusting chore.

TALE 2: WEIRD JEALOUSY

Daddy knew how "horse-obsessed" I was, and even though he was afraid of them himself, he went ahead and bought one for me. Because of the large size of the horse, we named him Big Boy, and he was almost seventeen hands! He was sweet-tempered and smart, but that changed over the summer.

As fall approached, I was getting new school clothes and supplies to prepare for the upcoming school year. This cut into the time I spent with Big Boy, and he was becoming surly.

When the bus started arriving each day for school, Big Boy reasoned out quickly that the bus was taking me away from him. I was gone all day, and he resented the bus.

He soon began to run alongside the bus (thank goodness for the sturdy fence that kept him in the pasture!), baring his teeth, flattening his ears, and snapping his teeth at the bus; he was trying to bite it!

We eventually had to sell him as he had become mean—even to me. I suppose he thought the bus driver and I were plotting against him.

TALE 3: CLEOPATRA AND COMPANY

One day, as I was about to get off the school bus, I heard really loud laughter and noticed the other kids pointing out the window. I couldn't imagine what was going on, but when I followed their gazes, I was so embarrassed!

Cleopatra (Mama was into historical names that year; we even had a steer named Napoleon), our huge mama hog, and her ten baby piglets had escaped their pen and were all, including Cleopatra, sitting upright like dogs and waiting at the bus stop for me. What a welcoming committee!

TALE 4: AN UNUSUAL FRIEND

Because we lived on a farm, people often would give us animals they no longer wanted, and we would gladly take them.

This is how Rocky came to be part of our lives. Rocky was a handsome young mynah with a delightful personality.

He slept in a brown paper lunch bag in his cage. When he was ready to turn in for the night, he would get into the bag by walking in backward, turning around a few times to settle in, and finally poking his head out to announce "Night, night" in a croaking voice

He also refused to eat normal bird cuisine but loved dry dog chow mixed with a little water. He would let you know he was finished with his meal by flinging it onto the wall, which quickly stuck and became like gravel; it was that hard to remove! We needed to be hypervigilant in getting to the chow before he did. Ha!

One warm spring day, Mama decided to let Rocky have a bath outdoors; it was his spa day. He loved this, and because his wings were clipped, he could not fly away.

He hopped into the pie plate, which was full of warm water, and set out on the porch. Busy with preening and fluffing out his feathers, he did not notice that he had company—our old cat, Tom. As Tom observed Rocky carefully, he began to go into his stalking mode. Slowly, he crept closer and closer to the bathing ritual.

Just as Tom was about to pounce, clever Rocky turned his head far to the side (his head was almost upside-down), looked at Tom, and said loudly, "Well, hello!" Poor Tom, he howled and took off as fast as he could go! He was gone for three days! I guess he wanted no part of a lunch that talked back.

TALE 5: A BITTER END—GOODBYE DUCKS

Some tales are sad, but this one should be included. You will soon see why.

One Sunday dinner, as we kids began heartily eating our delicious roast chicken, Mama began laughing. We were puzzled as nothing funny had happened, but we knew better than to ask what was going on.

She continued to laugh until we were all finished with the chicken, and then she said a terrible thing: "Don't ever tell me you don't like duck."

We were still baffled about what she meant. That's when we realized that she had killed and cooked our pet ducks, Heckle and Jeckle!

All of us kids immediately dropped our utensils and began to cry.

The even more bizarre thing was that to Mama, it was a joke, but to the rest of the family, including Daddy, it was heart-wrenching.

Decades later, I was watching the fine movie *Giant*, and when the scene came on about the family's pet turkey being served at their Thanksgiving meal, I was chilled. Did Mama get the idea from this movie scene? It was a monstrous thing to do to one's children, and even today, I am shaken by it.

TALE 6: END OF THE FARM

Our house was originally a barn, and while we loved living there, it was laid out strangely—as you can imagine. My brothers slept in what had been the hayloft, and the bedroom that my sister and I shared did not have a door; only a sheet covered the opening.

One night, we awoke to a terribly loud noise and a bright light shining through the wall next to our bed. A drunk driver had missed the curve, drove over an embankment, and crashed into our bedroom.

My sister and I were not hurt but were scared and confused.

My parents quickly bought another house, and we moved as soon as they sold the animals. They were very wise to move as that accident could have killed us both, and they were worried about another accident happening the same way.

ACKNOWLEDGMENTS

I would like to thank the many friends and strangers who have encouraged me to write my story. *Blessed beyond Measure* is their blessing upon me as well.

Over the years, whenever someone would hear only a small portion of my life's trials, they would be astounded. They would tell me that many people (women, men, and children) struggling with their lives would benefit greatly from reading such an account.

With this support behind me and constantly uplifting my spirits, I felt the love helping me along the way to completion. God has truly blessed me beyond measure.

Printed in the United States
by Baker & Taylor Publisher Services